It Says Here is Sean O'Brien's tenth book of poems.
His *Collected Poems* appeared in 2012. His work has received
awards including the T. S. Eliot and Forward Prizes, the Somerset
Maugham and the E. M. Forster Awards. His novel *Once Again
Assembled Here* was published in 2016 and his collection of short
stories *Quartier Perdu* in 2018. He is also a translator of works
including *The Birds* (2001), *Inferno* (2006) and Spanish Golden
Age plays by Tirso de Molina and Lope de Vega. He is Professor
of Creative Writing at Newcastle University and a Fellow
of the Royal Society of Literature.

Sean O'Brien

It Says Here

PICADOR

First published 2020 by Picador
an imprint of Pan Macmillan
6 Briset Street, London EC1M 5NR
Associated companies throughout the world
www.panmacmillan.com

ISBN 978-1-5098-4042-7

1 3 5 7 9 8 6 4 2

A CIP catalogue record for this book is available from the British Library.

Printed and bound by CPI Group (UK) Ltd, Croydon, CR0 4YY

In Memory of Michael McCarthy

In the end they are not spared. In their turn everything happens to them. Of any half dozen one has a secret vice, one an incurable disease, one a deep faith in God and the rest don't care one way or the other. But they see it happen.

Ken Smith, 'Part of the Crowd that Day'

Contents

It Says Here

It Says Here

That the way through the woods runs out in a blizzard.
That the ocean does not, is eternal,
And still for a while you may cross the great ice-dome
By dog-sled, though at your own risk.
That the book you are reading is one of a kind,
That its door opens inwards and cannot be closed.
That the train going over a bridge at night
Has somewhere to get to that even the driver,
Heroic and faceless and bathed in the heat
From the firebox, never discovers.
That the sky is a page where with a flourish
The birds write the truth in invisible ink
And the eye is too slow to be certain
That this word and that word are never to meet,
Or the poem will sicken and die.
That when you glance up from your reading
The rivers divide and divide till at last
You step down at a halt in the woods
With its name painted over,
And there in the evening the bride and the gamekeeper
Wait with their faces averted, wait
For the signal to shift and the lamp to glow red
And a train to arrive, but not yet and not yet.
That though this is August the snow is beginning.
You blink, and the woods are half buried
And the travellers gone, and as for the fire and the rose
That it now seems you set out in search of,
That is a different story, or so it says here.

I Found My Way

I found my way, the worse for drink,
Through petal-storms, the white, the pink.
The place was all significance —
The goddess in the jasmine's shade,
Sequestered in her green romance,
Arch on arch in deep recession.
Inaudibly the fountains played.

The seasons fled, as England slept
And I could not, a trespasser
On ground I'd owned. What business
Underwrote my being there?
Yet an appointment must be kept.
The roses, hooded for the frost
Like hangmen, saw that I was lost.

And yet this place was all I knew,
While how I came there and for what
Had never troubled me till now:
But now I walked that blessèd plot
Green avenue by avenue
Past royal rose and bergamot,
In residence yet passing through.

So what conclusion should I draw
From this arboreal baroque,
When every way led only here,
Whose silence waited like a clock?
And how should I enquire within
To learn the nature of the sin
For which I was arraigned? And then I saw:

This is the centre of the rose,
An empty sepulchre designed
To quench the tongue and close the mind,
The perfect, heartless, silent *o* –
She never cares to speak in prose –
Where there is neither *stay* nor *go*
Nor any means of saying so.

Three Songs

the memory of rain
falling into the water

the railway runs between
the wooded quarry and the river

high summer in the wood's throat
black and green, the brazen light

crackling with dryness where
returning only takes you further off

the air too still the pool long drained
and yet time haunts itself

and sees you as a ghost

*

my place that was low hills and marshes
grids of drainage winter floods

and once the story goes a Roman ford
all that was confiscated sown

with salt and caltrops
never had a name to call itself

from the poems of the era
you would learn responsibility

and the laconic scale that might
encompass the catastrophe

cities of brickdust and sewage
migration and the death of names

who cares it is a fact

*

in the soliloquy of Fortinbras
the soldier has most royally

put on his iron eloquence
as though he were a mercenary

in the employment of the facts
in the burning cities breakings on the wheel

burnt books the leisured relish
of annihilation places just like this

that in the scale of things can mean
precisely nothing till the armoured gaze

should pause above them on the map
the index finger point the iron mouth

be understood without the need of speech

Referendum

We posted ballots in absentia –
Three for the Miami Showband –
Due on at eight-thirty
And still sounding grand.

Asked Derry and the Romper Room,
Enniskillen and Omagh
To put the *x*'s in the boxes
Where all the bodies are.

We recalled the dead
From their state of disorder
And asked them to safeguard
The wide-open border.

Ave and *vale*
And how do you do?
Ten to a mile
They're waving us through.
Ten to a mile
They're waving us through.

If I May

The palace oh the palace and its undeserving opulence
Are not enough for some. There are episodes of stropulence.

A sealed coach slips the silver out in the disguise of night,
And at the torpid bourse the nation's capital takes flight.

There is talk of revolution, there are whispers of reform,
And anything seems possible except departure from the norm.

The mirrors on the miles and miles of aimless corridor
Are preparing their excuses. They have seen it all before.

M. le Dauphin – how to put this – well, sir, it is late.
The clerks are sneaking off and there are hangmen on the gate:
And at this hour, sir, you choose to sit and masturbate.

The Settembrini Bulletin

for Peter Porter

The creatures with the shears, whom you imagined
Spitting while they wait next door in Hell,
Have access to all areas. They come
As wonks and spads and black ops cybermen,
As keepers of the sweating corridors
With many ports but no way out.
They know our names and what we love.
Though you could not abide him, Dante shows
Damnation as a place of practicality,
Infernally productive – *we make pain* –
With every moment an eternity
Of manufacturing or services – and even
In the deepest vault, where Lucifer himself
Is nailed up on the wall of ice to weep
His river of unmelting tears, there's action
Of a sort, if there are witnesses: so cue
The poet and his psychopomp sent down
To do the job in depth and pacify the Muse
With product placement. Work or die?
Then best be doing in the daylight world –
Ergo the wetwork Barbariccias,
The whores and bailiffs helicoptered in
To clean up in between the massacres.
We've had enough of experts now, but still

You would have been at home, as though
This were a gallery where slaughter loans itself
To art's attention – 'No one seems worried
And the detail's beautiful', while out of shot
The leering creatures spit for England but
Since time is money will not stand and wait.

The Party

In the distance there sits the retired volcano
Blowing absent-minded smoke-rings,
Bent to the darkening book of the valley
That tells us its story of panthers and serpents
And roses forever, as if we were children.
Here at the party the beautiful women
Flicker like the long-ago *estrellas*
de cine, in monochrome Balenciaga,
Almost gone, still smiling on the men
Who will have everything and more,
The horses and the women and the moon
That rises from the dark caldera –
For desire, they will tell you gravely,
Is a duty much like death, its give and take.
Tomorrow is Ash Wednesday. The murderers
Will raise their scythes to join the carnival
Among the floats and masks and children
Dancing to the lakeshore. There at dusk
A coffin will be launched to bear away
The sins that flesh is heir to, free to drift
Until it beaches on the property of those
Who celebrate so grimly here tonight
The beauty of the women they have killed
And mean to kill, and the secret death of politics –
Which is, we learn, another name for sex,
The shallow graves and cellars where the monsters
Swim in blood to be reborn. And somehow

We are here with them, as if we've dreamed
Too long to wake. We ought to go. The horns
Strike up, timbales snap, and the assassins
Take their victims in their arms to make the moves
They've known since they were boys and girls.
It is the custom, and for us to vanish now
Would be discourteous. We join the ring
So smoothly we might be professionals.

Diu Nahtegal

Schöne sanc diu Nahtegal
    Vogelweide, 'Unter der Linden'

Schöne sanc diu Nahtegal
In the willow trees at dawn
By the Glienicker See
The blue song inexhaustible

If I could hear so could the Vopos
Nosing in their grim grey boat
Down among the rushes-oh
It was the shore of history

Another lake where legions drown
We told each other with no words
Schöne sanc diu Nahtegal
We told each other with no words

The saturated alphabet
Came flowing to no end at all
Schöne sanc diu Nahtegal
That history is for the birds

An Assignation

I will see you in the white square
Once again beneath the plane trees
By the church of St Eulalie.

It will be the middle of the afternoon
When everyone has disappeared
But you and I approaching secretly

By different streets. My life is
Nothing but this rendezvous, my love,
No past, no afterwards, only the breeze

That fidgets like a horse kept waiting
In that distant corner of the square,
Where I can see you now,

Already seated and expecting no one.
Your dress is blue, your book
Lies open by the empty glass you'll raise

As if in toast to no one while I pass
And raise in turn my non-existent hat
In token of this infinite commitment.

Farewell, then. Farewell. À demain.

Memento Mori

The old, since they are mad, think all the others mad
And all a good deal older than themselves, though this
Is relative, and most of them are relatives somehow.
Among these old and mad is one convinced by rage
That money knows no owner but herself, and thus
Is in the wrong hands certainly, and must be as it were
Retrieved, with blackmail as the righteous instrument,
According to her old mad lights. Meanwhile
In old mad Hampstead houses and in basement flats
Among the old mad Chelsea bombsites, life goes on
Signifying death in general, while the telephone
Provides a personal inflection when a voice
Adapted for each doomed recipient remarks
Politely: 'Now remember you must die.' Can these
Be human voices that awake the old and mad?
The great detective with his weakened heart thinks not.
To say 'Remember you must die,' and then ring off
Is not the kind of thing the well-heeled old and mad
Immured in their brown studies at their time of life
Prefer to hear, when there's still sex or money
To be dwelt on, where a child may visit on his makers
Complex economic loathing, and where all this weighs
Like bags of useless gold upon their injured hearts.
There is a private madhouse where an Irish lawyer
Called O'Brien thinks he's God. He sees His starry fields
Blaze cold against the velvet black of noon. So he's all right.

But up in town the slow disintegrating minds
Grind on like almost-immortality, and lights
Switch on and off in random circuits like the stars
Of a capricious heaven, as the servant plots her way
To minted doom, and time is money. Meanwhile death
Is all there is and more. This is a comedy.

Hyperbole

You might think you're talking about history.
Or politics. You're talking about poetry.
Likewise with art and love and death or guilt
Or loss – you're talking poetry. I mean it.

For the world, dear friend, is full of pretexts
And occasions whose disguise
Is that they look like meanings when in fact –
Need I go on? We'll say no more about it.

Archonography

Sean Scully: Inset 2

Believe you me, we understand the urge
To rectify. So much is chaos, so much
Mere filler to surround the thrust of things

Across the next horizon. So then, let
The field be unified, each part the whole.
Let ground be figure; figure, ground.

We can foresee – but somehow in reverse –
An empire's late cartography in this,
Minute and rectilinear, layered on itself

As if to charge and frame a sudden depth
That has no room for cities such as ours,
Nor for the names of those who build

And bring them low. Here geometry
Is God in all but name, and where we stand
And what we stand on must be nothingness,

Which leaves us with the meantime
In the latticework of 'ordinary life', to reach
Across the gulf, as though we ever could.

There is an art to this, as absolute
And terrible as politics or music,
And it must be very late, the harmonies

About to shriek themselves apart,
The old simplicities, the muted greens
And browns of pastoral retirement

Long dead but honoured in the parody.
Much more of this and we'll have neither
History nor grievance, cause nor consolation.

So for a moment you delight us, yet
Whichever dispensation operates,
The corridors by which you came

Lead only here, to this small chamber
Where, when you've been shown the instruments,
We put you to the question once again.

An American Activity

For Tamar Yoseloff

As a boy I read the death that Roethke dreamed of:
Running out of road, and then the vehicle stalling
As the windscreen filled with snow.
It stayed with me, that resting-place,
Although in time the car itself became confused
With other wrecks from Dickey and Dave Smith,
Where kudzu coiled like sex among the rusted springs.
Today I find the poem again: now Yeats and Stevens
Look on unamused at Roethke's borrowed robes.
And yet that piety he carried like insurance
To the snowy ditch, to the cliff at world's end,
To the garden men of forty glimpse at dusk
When opening the icebox for the lonely sake of it,
Has never lost its hold, although it wasn't meant for me.
This is their birthright, lodged like a minié ball
In a skull at Antietam, a grammar of train-whistles
Heard across the hills a hundred years
And more ago, and never headed here.
No place for me, though I am occupied by listening
To a music that can scarcely know itself
And yet meets all occasions: thus they gather at the river,
They return from foreign wars to ignorance and scorn,
They take their turns at parenthood, at burying their own
And at divorce, and − it is evening − come to stand

And watch a baseball diamond left to elegize
Stage four of its neglect, between two railroad yards
While fighting drunks steal bases from their skeletons.
What competence and what complacency:
How inextricable the habit that was there
Before the habits formed, that always knows
A pathway through the woods and past the fatal creek
To find the crazy widow's shotgun shack awaiting
Immortality. The hidden way is marked at every turn,
Secure in all the righteousness that makes
Life look like religion and religion look like them.
These men who at fifty fall for sophomores,
These women who will put themselves to death
In the assault on greatness, cannot be denied
Their place among the saints. As well exclude the air itself
Or dam the smoking waters where they flow
Through burning forests and exhausted plains:
And why should anyone do that, they'd turn and ask,
Supposing they were listening. It is the right of all
To be a headlamp on a northbound train,
Or, lifting up their hearts unto the hills,
To sing of death as if it were a clause
Revoked in secret from the Constitution
And replaced with other words, like these.

Names

Ravenspur, Ravensrodd, Ravenser Odd,
Salt-heavy bells heard only by God.

Drink to the lost and the longshore drift:
When there is nothing the names will be left.

HAMMERSMITH

'Fierce warres and faithful loves shall moralize my song.'

Canto I

England is finished, not that it matters
When even the weather is done for,
When the Boat Race ends though it's barely begun,

With a boy from Wisconsin who catches a crab.
For a moment the eye has him
Over and gone in the silver-black Thames,

In the deep shade of Harrods Depository –
Drowned Palinurus to sleep with the fishes
And raggedy scuttlers down on the slime-bed,

And several books later converse with John Snagge
In the slow fields of Hades by Hammersmith Bridge
Where Richard Widmark also met his end

At the climax of *Night and the City*, that love-song
To water and terror and death –
Oh, but the oarsman recovers, though the race is lost

By a shaming ten lengths, with ill-tempered
Un-boating appeals to the pitiless umpire,
An agent of Mercury, surely, by which time

I'm losing my faith in this annual fiction,
The same way as Aintree and Wembley
Can no longer tell me my name when I wander

From Hammersmith boozer to boozer and stand
In the jittery shade of the London planes
At the corner of King Street and Beadon Road

In 1960 or in 1945 or now, where I tell
Anybody who knows me and many who don't:
I was more or less born here and woke to the sound

Of a wireless commentary, all England gathered
In its draughty living room to hear itself
Made language in the voice of Mordaunt Snagge.

All lies, as we neither affirm nor deny.
I was an old believer in that sound
Before the smell of valves and burning dust

Gave way to class, the major stench of things.
Do try to take more water with it, love.
It used to be all pubs round here

When my mother would walk out to dances,
The war lately over and the streets awash
With the Irish, among them her blue-eyed undoing.

– Thus Ryan, astray in the four-ale bars
Sees history invent itself
Between the blue smoke and the ceiling

And the pages of the sporting calendars,
Between one sentence and the next
When one door closes, then another

And the girl is gone in a cymbal-crash,
A nurse, a teacher, left no name
And the only game is a young man's game,

The quickstep and the Palais glide
And the invitation to step outside.
And she'll sit this one out if it's all the same.

The world is beginning where it ended,
With the evening street and the London plane
Leprous and beautiful, meant for rain.

If you lose yourself in Parson's Green
Then ask Our Lady to intervene
Blue is the heaven and dark is the sky

Lady be with us for now we die
Thus Ryan, in the trap of elegy.
Nor am I out of it, excepting insofar

As it became habitual
After such a promising beginning.
Off the Irish train at Euston,

Brilliantined, with mostly original teeth
And a past that I shall not go into again.
In the street there is a door

And past the door the stairs go up
And up into the dark, up
To a final room for rent that shows

A hundred rain-blue roofs and other rooms,
A park that hurries out of sight –
The wind at dusk applies the whip –

And the risen moon presiding from afar.
Oh loneliness, your name is Hammersmith.
The river fills again, the barges wake and shift

On skating blackness. Now would be the time
To find her coming to the dance
Among a crowd of other girls, the time to know

This room, the empty stairs, the empty street,
The high tide of the gale,
As an annunciation.

England is gone, with snoek and the ground-nut scheme,
With Aneurin Bevan and Stafford Cripps
And the cold coming of immigrant ships,

To decline and fall, to a wind of change
To a world no longer rich and strange
Where Caliban and Ariel

Shivered at the sound of the sunset bell
At Lloyd's and at Evensong's white chill
And the citizen army cobbled its boots

For the money had long run away down the drain.
Do you love an apple, do you love a pear,
Do you love the boy with the curly brown hair

For it's still I love him, I can't deny him
I'll be with him wherever he goes

Canto II

Once more you emerge in the autumn light
To find your parents' London gone
From the streets where the gasping buses grind on

To no fixed abode, where is no stay,
Not known at this address,
Or never known, or went away,

Gone where the post eventually goes,
With the midnight flit or the number
Forgotten for want of a pencil just then

On the dim top landing or under a streetlight
At closing. In this way their city is lost
With all the lives they might have led.

You want to go home. But you have to begin.
Here now at noon you must empty the Broadway
Of all but the dead, and set out

From the unquiet shade of the plane-trees
As if you must know where you're going,
As if you might even belong.

The world for which the nation fought admits
No Blacks and no dogs and no Irish,
And yet you see a room somewhere,

And still in a cupboard over a sink
A bottled hint of brilliantine, as might
Be applied to an evening in prospect.

Then girls on the edge of the dancefloor
Settle their cardigans over their shoulders,
And close their handbags with a snap

To indicate several places to be
And not for the good of their health, dear me.
Now what will it be? Will we wait and see?

Then the band strikes up and away you go.
Am I haunting you now? Are you there?
Away they go under the railway arch

And into the hinterland, streets behind streets,
The dead go dancing on silent feet,
Over the wall into Ravenscourt Park,

Down frosty pathways and into the dark –
With a strange resemblance to happiness or
With a resolution to settle for less,

As the price of a kiss? Was it for this
That Ryan discovers himself on these streets,
Uncertain whether to laugh or cry?

The big-band silence, the make-do-and-mend
And the demob suits and the Palais Glide
And the Mick and his girl from the North Countree?

The dancers are gone. The bus rolls by.
Ryan recovers himself on the street
With a nightmare thirst and aching feet,

In need of something resembling repose
And a pint of black to re-enchant
A world that is always and only prose,

To offset the fear of what you might find,
Whatever it is that lies behind
The heartless song of the District Line

High over the secret far end of the street,
That says every verse-end that the here and now
Is neither here nor there, and that

If there is life it must happen elsewhere.
Look now, Ryan, in the *A to Z*,
For the nowhere to which your enquiries have led –

A pub that was fading, then boarded, then sold,
Too far from the river, too far from the shops,
An in-between place where the calendar stops,

A site for a starlet's final berth
In a flat whose windows are touched with gold
When at teatime September is suddenly cold

On the dim, dusty fringes of Hammersmith.
Now you have come to the ends of the earth.
What is there now but the water's edge?

The barges shift as the river awakes
And the painters at work on the green-gold bridge
Stare down as the black tide tightens its grip.

Why not let it take you away?
Here there is nowhere. Here is no stay.
The streetlights blink and the air-brakes sigh.

The barmaid knows what the problem is.
It's your *modus vivendi*, she silently says.
If you lean out to look, it's easy to slip.

You sit at the bar that is no longer there,
As the click of her high heels over the parquet
Resolves to a quickstep and out of the door

To a smouldering street at the end of the war.
Remember now, Ryan, you have an engagement.
So Ryan reads poems. Who gives a fuck?

Demented abuse from the not all there,
A bitter wee Jock with rodent-red hair –
See Apologia? Don't even start –

Makes absolute sense of a dying art.
It is night now, and autumn, high tide.
So, Ryan, why at the slightest excuse

Must you look for a sign? You will fail
Like your father before you to speak
The true name of these waters. He left you

His life, in an all-too exemplary suitcase –
Poems and politics, no fixed address –
A suitcase brim-full of the waters of Lethe

And, for the ulcer, Belladonna, which way
Madness lay in wait for him, and yet
You will lower your face to the water,

And through it, and open your eyes.

Canto III

A lifetime upriver, out here on this spindly bridge
Across the sky-blue Cherwell
I watch the flat earth mirror heaven

In the February flood. Can it be that now
On the brink of old age I may begin?
The dreaming mind will lose no chance

To mobilize belief, so why not here
Among the sunken willows
And the houseboats moored to nowhere –

'Our lives in infinite preparation'?
                                        Did you ever
Take a notion, Ryan asks, *to jump in the river and drown?*
I think we're drowned already.
                                        Eighty years upriver

I think of her in a borrowed gown,
Sneaked in by a friend to hear Tolkien
Or Lewis – to feel that for an hour she knew

The place she was intended for until the war.
Then she walked on Port Meadow
And over this bridge and around, and she saw

When she gave back the gown that this
Must be afterwards, final, that life was denied
And would have to go on, since anyway

What can you do, as she'd say, but get on with it?
Therefore she teaches. Her home is the war.
At evening she walks by the river, rehearsing her lines

For the Players. She will be Juno
While you-know-who will be Joxer. A prophecy.
The pressure wave had killed them all

Where they sat at the table, quite unmarked
And with their evening meal before them
She tells you the story from time to time

Till sixty years are gone, and still the family
Are seated there, as though to contemplate
A kind of leisure life would not permit

And death itself cannot remember.
And although I cannot see their faces,
Now, as her memory goes, I must

Believe it for her: the pan of spuds
Still rippling from the blast, while she
Has lines to learn, and books to mark,

An eye to keep on you-know-who.
She walks by the river to get it by heart.
The water is her *aide-memoire*. I dare to think

It can remember her when she is gone,
Calm and preoccupied, nose in a book
Or turned aside to watch the garden grow,

Beside the water's *roman fleuve* –
A making-sense that makes no sense
Except in passing, as the teams of oarsmen

On the calm of their creation glide
With the insane accomplishment of insects
Under the bridge and out of sight,

The wordless urgings of their coaches
Following, and the river's reach extending
Down from Chiswick Mall to the blazing slums

Behind the docks, and back by dawn.
A making-sense that makes no sense
Except in passing. I watch as the waters

Part and rejoin at the Eyot. They are passing
Away from the world she knew and I am dreaming
To remember, where the dead sit patiently

As though a daughter's late again
And yet expected, loved, provided for,
With the wireless dead where history ends

In the indefinite suspension
Of fixtures I supposed were England always.
Learn the script, she says, then mark the books.

Believe in chalk and talk and human kindness
Whatever the evidence says. Speak up.
There's always work to do among the dead.

New gaps in the register week after week,
Times of which she'll hardly speak,
Though you know she had only a pencil and chalk

With which to bring enlightenment
To forty East End boys who did not think
They needed saving but in time

Were all converted, giving her in turn
The faith in chalk and talk, stern sympathy
And in the virtue of persistence

In itself, there being no reward but that.
She walks by the river and learns her lines
To spar with you-know-who. A prophecy.

Canto IV

Left under the bed in a suitcase
Flat ephemeral pamphlets of an era
More remote than Troy or Carthage.

What shall we wish for, hope for, serve?
The means of production, comrade.
And having once secured it, get

The English out of England finally.
In case of fire, put on more coal.
But of course you were hoping for more,

The real thing all the fuss and smoke
And misery deserved to be about.
You go down the slick steps of the well

To emerge in the dark at low tide
Where the luminous pages of all his drowned books
Set out like stepping stones across the mud

In all directions and in none.
The ur-text is *Mulligan*, lost in transit,
The big one, yes that one, of which survives only

A rumour of your man's nocturnal
Riparian bench-talk, lost between tides
On the fogbound / the starlit / the frozen /

The flooded embankment: rumoured aesthetics of Mulligan,
Small change of Mulligan, dead trousers alleged
Of said Mulligan, poet of no fixed abode

Or home team, one *soi-disant* 'Mulligan',
Apostrophizer of the moon, mud-mutterer
For whom says Mulligan the state intends

An utter absence from the lists
By confiscation of the name itself:
No Mulligan here, ergo

Un-Mulligan: bear in mind also
That firstly others will decide who
May be called Anonymous, and secondly

It won't be you, for yea the very imprint
Of the planking of this handsome bench
Upon the non-existent arse of nobody

Who never sat on this embankment
Shall herewith be effaced by governmental magic.
It's Mulligan never: it's Mulligan not: it's no Mulligan here.

And if still a voice will almost surface
From the candid foolscap put away
In the suitcase for later, the lifetime of later,

Have suitcase will travel, will slowly unravel
And at last *go mad that way*, it is only
The ill-starred prodigious inaudible Mulligan,

Derelict, dead in the water, a drifter
Asking to be scuttled, set ablaze, struck off
At Lloyd's and the Vatican, by National Insurance

And even for good brutal measure, God knows,
By the Royal Antediluvian Order of Buffaloes.
Begun and re-begun, a paper cell of theological

Devising, where he must *re-enter and re-enter*
Under the gaze of the Black and Tan sergeant
Who is there to meet him always

When he looks up from the page and back
And finds it still unwritten and the sergeant
With his 'teeth like washing-boards',

Attentive at the spyhole of the cage.
Imagine me, the sergeant says, *imagine me*
You fucking taig. Imagine that.

Canto V

Beneath the East River, there lie in wait
Tunnels, ladders, hatches and the friend
Whose legs were amputated by a train.

You told me once you were deported,
But never how these elements combine.
So long now among the anecdotes, like you

I find the facts are neither here nor there –
The child in love with maps and lithographs
Finds everywhere a match for appetite:

But though it's infinite beneath the lamp,
As memory the world sails out of sight –
And nor am I, if I can see the worklights,

Scaffolding knee-deep in water, the *mise-en-abîme*
Where girders sweat, and any second now
A disaster site or the scene of a crime you may

Only just have departed. Or dreamed, like me,
The second son you thought you'd never have,
To whom you lent the name you gave the first.

There is a darkness in your mind that means
You cannot read a novel for yourself
And dare not care for music. It's as though

You came into the world with barely half a kit,
Or else are one who lost a life elsewhere
And cannot make it home [again]. I see you

Passing down the tunnel like a ghost
Who cannot find his level of damnation.
– Then nothing, and the friend is never named

And you can never quite be placed, although
You surface briefly in Southampton
Like a rumour spread by rumour,

As if you were a story, with a plot
Or even understanding to impart.
Lately I've been watching *Ocean Terminal*

And a page of Baudelaire appears
On a desk in a shipping office, magnified
By oceanic lenses, words themselves

Alone, transported from the world alone,
And now, among the long-dead reefs of paper
In this room that turns to nowhere, I can read

A version of that language still,
Inert with promise, as at last, for all
The lies and geography, we proved to be.

The child in love with maps and lithographs
Finds everywhere a match for appetite:
But though it's infinite beneath the lamp,
As memory the world sails out of sight.

One morning we embark. The mind ablaze,
The heart blown up with rancour and disease,
We set out with the rhythm of the tide,
Infinitude adrift on finite seas.

Some do it to escape the hated State;
Some flee the horrors of indoors, and some –
Stargazers blinded by a woman's stare –
Outrun the lure of Circean perfume,

And rather than be beasts consign themselves
To space and light and skies of molten brass,
Where biting cold and heat that roasts them black
Will slowly mask the imprint of her kiss.

But the authentic travellers are those
Who, light as balloons, take off and never give
Consideration to the claims of fate
And, never asking why, demand to live.

Such men's desires map themselves in clouds.
They dream the way a squaddie dreams a gun,
Of unknown pleasures, protean and vast,
Out where the writ of language cannot run.

Canto VI

The river in her low-tide ruination,
Ramparts of mud with oozy slakes
To feed the trench. Something is done with,

Mulligan says, so make your peace
With the impedimenta, moon and bridge
And whatever is the past or not. You need

A sense of occasion to suit the low
Admonitory brass that follows Gustav Holst
On his perambulations through the night,

While Mulligan goes widdershins –
How it takes in the faintest curdled merriment –
Mechanicals with walk-ons, at the dancing, at the bar,

Embracing the far end of night when they can sense
The waters quicken in the river's mouth
And actions having consequences: so.

They treat the river as themselves,
Unknowable and intimate, at hand yet out of reach.
Respect them in their ragged tableau vivant:

They build the city; they damn it, dream it, call it theirs
And walk the streets without a by-your-leave
And give it people. All you are is here,

Just out of reach, inaudible, the sound of frost
Among the cobblestones, as the darkness
Passes over the secret night-water,

A poster in a workshop underneath the railway
For a play, a dance, a palais of varieties.
– Now will that do you? Night and the city,

The music you have to imagine. My failure
Like my lousy teeth I leave to you
In perpetuity, if I could just pronounce it.

And oh important documents. Imagined futures
Obsolete *avant la rêve*. This poem
I stand accused of almost having written –

Left luggage at a station no one mentions nowadays.
And where the photographs and letters ought to be,
An emptiness that smells of brilliantine.

The living think there's something owed to them:
It's what they have in common with the dead.
A night bus slows on the bridge chicane.

The dozing riders stare out at themselves
Against the dark. The trench is filling silently.
They'll come for me, the dead watch, out from trees

And lamp-posts, tireless, at walking pace.
You will not save me then, or understand
The nature of my torment, since my past

Does not exist. This is not solitude but something worse.
Better I were indigent and drowned
Beneath the bridge, my son, than you should find

My bare convictions wanting as the rest have done.
Your fate, like mine, is to imagine otherwise.
It is not solitude but something worse, to know

That men are only wolves and devils
And I am somehow of their party.
Look in the suitcase. Take up and flick through

A *flat ephemeral pamphlet*,
Wishful as a tooth beneath a pillow. Socialism
Proved too good for us. It asked too much.

The revolutionary's Olivetti
Lies beneath its crust of fag-ash
Like a relic of Pompeii.

This is not solitude but something worse.
Carbon paper always looks
Pre-emptively incinerated, and *held*

One moment burns the hand.
I look over his shoulder as he types:
Nothing to eat and nowhere to sit down.

One story and one story only,
The mad priest / traveller / deserter
Gone to ground in the deserted village

To discover he was Satan all along. Two pages
On a good day. Finish it, my mother says,
Not looking up from where she marks

A thousand scripts while smoking, knitting,
Re-reading *The Daughter of Time.*
Other days a single sentence

Made, re-made, abandoned while the freezing fog
Descends and we are once more back
In the romantic cul-de-sac

Designed to suit a firing squad
And not to house a lightning-rod.
Thesis, antithesis, months of labour

In the History Room with fake stained-glass
And panelling, and heads of Silenus
Carved into the fireplace, and the smoke

From all those Player's Plain
A blue heaven where the lightning brewed.
But poems, what poems? Never a one.

This is not solitude but something worse.
Expelled from every diary and archive
As from the barest anecdote, the exile

Left no place to lose or wish for lingers
As an absence, less than shadow, on the fringe
Of doctored photographs that prove

The exigencies of the day exceeded
The technology: so there he's not, and yet
As blatant as the mastermind's cheroot

Self-smoking in the ashtray when the panel
In the fireplace closes silently while an entire
Continent of tunnels floods with sand

To make from mere evasiveness a myth
That we will never hear about. Such vast
Machinery should serve the supernatural,

Should be the adamantine ampersand
That binds the merely human to the gods.
Says Ryan, but all you leave me are these streets

You might have walked, as if they're evidence
Of how it was to try and fail at politics
And poetry and love and in the end

Become a dead man walking, followed
By the dead police who tracked you down
From false address to false address,

To destitution and beyond,
And when you turned to take them on, became
Mere London planes and lamp-posts once again,

Then crowded in the bathroom mirror,
Fingers to their lips, your gaolers once again.
There was nowhere to go, so there you went.

Again I was come back he went, you liked to say,
As if this too were secret
What mere economy could save you then,

Again I was come back he had went, you liked to say,
The glass in which I will not find you
Now or ever?

Canto VII

Remember this? No? Look again.
This is the only place you've ever been.
Drowned in the mirror of the dim afternoon,

In the irreparable betweentimes, bookies vanished
And the mind dried out with waiting, this is the life.
The patient failures glance up intermittently:

If nothing else, a drinker may catch his own eye
And return the slightest nod, as a conspirator
Might look back from the screen

Into this dappled sunken light-and-bitter bar
That never closes if your face is known, the place
The meantime goes to die. The slightest nod.

The barmaid looks up from her *Photoplay*. A death occurs.
When they run for the boats in *The Red Berets*
My half-imaginary cousin Patric Doonan meets his end

As Flash, a cheery cockney keen on skirt.
He turns to give covering fire. He falls
And Alan Ladd and Leo Genn and Harry Andrews

Live to jump another day and never mention Flash again.
He climbs from an unmarked grave to take his wage
And drink away the afternoons, perhaps to coincide

With Joxer on the lash, but finds himself at last
Uncredited in 1958 in Chelsea with a choice
Of bigamy or death and switches on the gas.

An underrated piece of realism, before its time
And thus too late. He is not spoken of.
Death is scarcely a rumour in here. Death is nobody's business,

A different class of a thing in a different district,
Far scream of a siren, scream of a train,
A single line of monorhyme.

See, no one in here is a part of the main.
No one in here is in here at all excepting
Those the afternoon has made immortal.

Time pauses to consider and forgets
What it came for, and one of the sleepwalkers
Raises the piano lid to strike a sour note.

What d'you think you're playing at? the barmaid snaps.
Who are you then? Hoagy Carmichael?
Now there's Uncle Jack on the back of a lorry

Delivering a tonic to the troops. He was among the first
To enter Belsen and did not recover. His piano
Haunts successive rooms, his widow's pre-fab

And his daughter's house, for neither wants
To let it go. By night you hear how it rehearses
In the silence of discretion, like a pianola

With its paper tongue cut out. The aunts
Do not approve of history: one day you see
Their own grandparents' trunk from Mafeking

And then you don't. *Oh it was full of worm.*
You wouldn't want to keep a thing like that –
It's like that damn piano, always there

And in the way. Out of the grave their father
Rises to his work, and he is not what you were told,
A porter at the hospital, but rather an attendant

At the workhouse. Thus the poor corral the poor.
There is a power that invests us with the longing
To forbid. It is the grey attention in the air

Of rented passageways, door after door,
Next flight, half-landing, skylight, blue-black heaven
Where the moon makes clear

That it can promise nothing.
Dare say. Very likely. No nothing at present.
No place like home since home is nowhere.

Yet you rise from the grave of yourself
To this long afternoon in the four-ale hell
Which admits no before and no after

'*And where he must re-enter and re-enter,*'
A private cinema of thirst and failure
With the same thing always showing,

Real as you and her yet quite untouchable.
The hand that you extend will pass
Into the mirror where the congress of accusers

With their teeth like washing-boards
Is assembled in the flooded cellar
So that you may reach the truth together

In the cause of *épuration. Are you true?*
A girl and a gun is the rule
And comrade you have neither. So as it were

Naked I / you entered the conference chamber.
That was a close one. A blast from the past
That raised a stench of gas and sewage

In the deserted street where you stand
Blinking in the chilly teatime sunset,
One of those *creeks of London silence*

[54]

By the water's edge. Now let the dark assurance
Carry you away once more. *Come home with me.*
Come down the water-stairs and come aboard. The waters

Braid and shudder, braid and shiver, parting at the pillars of the bridge.

Canto VIII

Eighty years upstream from Hammersmith
On the edge of a nondescript field
That shades off into birch and hawthorn –

Never mind groves: this is barely a place –
There in the hummocks of winter-white grass
(I see what is not there or anywhere)

There lies a mouth forever opening
To discharge a stream of language wedded
To the slur and swallow of the water, in a tongue

As limpid as the speech of nightingales
And silent as the grave's aphasia. Listen
And you almost hear it almost speak.

The fault is yours as much as any
Saturnine conjunction of the stars.
You leaned your back against that door

And fell straight down the cellar stairs
Into the pool of darkness standing there,
Illimitably patient in its cave.

And when you climbed back dripping to the light
You couldn't spit it out, just what it was
That you imagined you were playing at.

Since when the daylight swells and wavers.
Dust-motes in a shaft of sunlight hang
Suspended like the chalk that never settles

In the glass you raise and raise until you choke,
That cannot quench your lack but deepens it
With every swallow. Drowned already.

Who are you to raise the dead, require
The truth of them or make *lachrimae rerum*
Run dry? Or like Procrustes fit them

To a history they could not know was taking place
There on the wireless, there on the bus,
There when a woman took time to powder her face

And arrive at a separate peace.
These people have a right to leave
The faintest outline on the air and die.

Turn a deaf corner and the buses blare
Beneath the flattened thunder of the flyover
And glasses rattle on the shelves of bar-rooms

Sleeping off the night before. The tide of murk
Descends into itself again. The houseboats settle,
Jury-rigged at the pontoons forever,

As figures from Ravilious emerge on deck
To water the chrysanthemums displayed
In fire-buckets on the cabin roofs

As if this were the prospect of the future –
Demi-pastoral in cardigans with jazz,
While round the corner bombsites flower

With fireweed and Britain falls to Churchill
In a peaceable Dunkirk from sheer exhaustion,
Though the numbers do not lie. That year

The Oxford boat will sink; the re-staged race
Sees Cambridge winning: there on bikes and balconies
Along the Mall the crowding phantoms of festivity

Have not stopped cheering and can see no reason
Not to live this afternoon forever.
Where are Juno and Joxer in this picture?

Not quite gone, though time in their world shortens
Like the odds. November comes and those
Who built the Skylon tear it down again,

A Festival – a past – abolished with a bonfire
Raining ash into the river like a war
In miniature, lest we recall

What might have been had England kept the faith
So many had professed in one another.
The play is done, the sets are struck, the hall

Has always staged this empty silence. Overnight
The words of Fry and Duncan cease to be
Anachronistic and instead were never here.

So too the lodger with a single suitcase
Leaves the room as bare as ever and the landing
With its smell of soup and death

Immutably indifferent. Gone under the river
To build a new tunnel, gone over the hill, gone home
To no fixed address. Not known, except

That I know, though I'm desperate to forget,
The awful hopefulness of poverty
Averted by a day, an inch, a wash

And a decent shave, a district like the one escaped,
With evening bar-rooms in their palls of smoke
And jobs that might exist if x remembers.

I come looking for the exit. Not down here
Along these flooded corridors knee-deep
In Chronicles and Heralds. Not in this

Abandoned labyrinth where smoke and water fuse
And pinups leer and if ever cowards fled
Then it was *all so unimaginably different and all*

So long ago. That's no excuse, says Ryan.

Canto IX

It is far away, sixty years later.
This dying city's leaking steam
From every joint. The libraries are closed,

The discards burning in the mayoral hearth,
And out along the ragged edge
The book of January is white at dawn

Like the long field under hoarfrost
That divides this old estate
On which no library ever stood

And where the poor are exiled now.
To ignorance and rickets.
You cannat eat a poem, canny lad.

Past the full, the tall moon
Climbs aboard its long farewell,
And from the coldest depths

A dog might hear the peal of star-clouds
In the moment of extinction.
At this late stage we find

A promise in these distant facts
When scale must serve for sacrament.
And after all, this book of January

Remains unwritten, does it not?
Why should its pages not record
The works and days of hands like these

Before they perish from the earth?
Here come the early walkers now
To vanish down desire paths

Across the clear, new-published
Whiteness, with white voices raised
As if this field of tall, enormous cold

Was once upon a time a chamber
Where the poor could get a hearing
In a parliament of frost, with words

That might bear scrutiny,
And even now, without recourse,
Perhaps not even memory itself,

They keep a kind of faith
With rumours of a Silver Age
By shouting as they meet and part

And disappear. Ten minutes
See them on their way
From zero hours to graveyard shift.

If they would truly wish it still,
Beyond the habit of forgetfulness
There is another story to be told.

And yet. And yet the book of January
Is having none of it.
I am a text whose only page

Is white, it says. *I am a book of breath,*
That freezes for a moment and is gone.
I've spent my life accumulating books

I now discard for want of space –
Or maybe inclination, since that faith
Seems founded on the air in which it melts.

And yet it's cold, and men once more
Become the wolves they always were.
Juno, Joxer, after '47, after '63,

You would think this is scarcely a winter at all,
But it bites, till the spirit considers itself
An illusion bred out of a settlement

None but the powerless believe in now.
There are people, if you can believe them,
Who think it is nostalgia saying so,

And that we have no history,
While by the logic of their frankness, they
Themselves are scarcely there: cold weather

Thins them down until you see straight through
To the graveyard they will build on next.
Juno and Joxer, tell me: what am I

Contracted to except the past, the solitudes
I cross in search of you? What am I but the tale
You did not think that you were telling?

Canto X

At the end of the garden runs a river
I will never reach. They walk there
In the silence of the intimate, and with the day

So vast and patient they have nothing on the clock.
I come indoors and light the fire
And look up at the flickering leer

On the face of Silenus carved over the mantel.
The old are sent here from the future
To ensure that we despair.

Better never to have been, but failing that
Stick to aesthetics, which in turn
Will stick to you like napalm. Thus Ryan.

Deep beneath the hearth a beam is smouldering,
Ignited by a memory that leaves the city
Mined with unexploded ordnance

Sunk among the bones in flooded graves.
Re-reading Captain January and Braddock by the fire
I am part, still, of the done war.

The old weight-bearing beam consumes itself
Austerely, by the splinter, in a steady, tended rage
Whose day will come and look like vindication

When the stack of storeys falls into itself
And through itself, and down again
And down, through the final dark river to nowhere,

For underneath this fury that will seek
Its own extinction in the wreck
Of all that stands and call it victory,

There is no bedrock to be found.
Imaginary England
Rises for a moment like a gas-flare

From a sewer and is gone.
Now leave me with the house divided
To await its immolation, to bear witness here,

Complicit by the fact of being born
And drinking from the poisoned well.
Let books and earth and oily water burn,

Likewise the living and the dead,
But let me remember the possible days,
The river, where the garden ends

And those I lost are walking still.

Little Pig Finnegan

The alternative version

The farmer was talking
And Little Pig Finnegan
Heard what the farmer had said
That one's tail is too straight
And there's no time to wait
So he's going for bacon instead tra la
He's going for bacon instead

When your pig saw his ass
In a large looking-glass
The farmer had not been mistaken
Young Finnegan boked
At the thought he'd be smoked
And he felt all alone and forsaken
I'm going for bacon instead tra la
I'm going for bacon instead

But his big sister Bridget –
That's Biddy for short –
Said you'll be for breakfast
If ever you're caught
So I'm putting these mints
In this bundle I've brought
Now run away Finnegan

Run run away
On your little pig legs
Or you'll be the bacon
That goes with the eggs
The bacon that goes with the eggs tra la
The bacon that goes with the eggs

So Finnegan fled
With a price on his head
(Or in fact on his little straight tail)
Away far away
Till the breaking of day
When he came to a farm
A wee place of great charm
Where the farmer's wife beckoned him in tra la
Where the farmer's wife beckoned him in

She fed him and bathed him
And fed him again
Till the sleep rose up over his head
She put on a white coat
And she cut his wee throat
Till he thought holy fuck now I'm dead tra la
Till he thought holy fuck now I'm dead
Then she minced him for sausage instead tra la
She minced him for sausage instead

The Trespasser

I had forgotten the fidelity with which
You beat the bounds of the estate
You think is yours and yet is not.

Likewise your fury at the trespasser
Who comes and goes and does not care,
Whose merest wish unlocks a private gate.

You were not called; nor were you sent.
There is no one you represent.
Now tend your rage in private, please.

Switch out the lights. Hand in your keys.
You are not who, nor are you where
You may suppose. You're not all there.

The Long Field

Late summer still, just barely. People are away
The long field's mown. The aspens wait
For the wind to bring rain. And when it comes
Rain has itself for company this afternoon –
The roar, the hush, the sudden afterwards
When everything looks round as though
Awoken from exhausted wakefulness.
We are old now, you tell me. The lives we have led
Lead here, to this hour after the rain.
We have tried to be those on whom nothing is wasted
While knowing that all this is merely the case,
As the pronouns are, or those dim figures
Swimming up with neither names nor dates,
The decorative impulse gone to seed,
Delivering their gifts of obligation to recall
The place, the year, inconsequent and labyrinthine.
The sound of the Metro hangs in the wind.
Late afternoon, with its sensible emptiness.
Fresh clouds come gliding in from westwards
On columns of cross-hatch on cross-hatch.
When the rain begins again, the horses
Move in slowly underneath the trees as if
Not quite invited, left out by the travellers
To wait with a tin bath of leaves and black water.
Is it a sacred mystery, this mere contingency?
It places you beside me, reading at the window,
Breaking off to comment, deaf to the clock.

Why not? If I could I would live here forever,
Feeding my redundant papers to the flames.
But there's the far-off clatter of the Metro
Veering suddenly much closer, like a carriage
On the Ghost Train hurtling into view –
While we are watching fifty years ago
With brandy-snap and inarticulate desires –
Then plunging back behind the double doors
Into the night where girls are screaming.
Somewhere in there is a hairpin bend
Where a skeleton station-master waits,
His fob-watch nesting in his finger-bones.
Where was I? Siding with the elements
That take no sides. Let's close the window now
But oh forget me not, forget me not.
Let's watch the rain emulsify and slide
Across the glass that holds our faces,
Carefully committing them to memory.

Cicadas

We watch the sea below. It seems to be our task
To keep in mind this blue mirage with no horizon,
Neither wine nor water though we'd drink it if we could
In search of somewhere else like this but not like this.

The olive trees condense dry shadow-pools
To stand on in the burning groves. And there is music
Of a sort, when the cicadas once more
Strike up the rehearsal. They are serial amnesiacs.

Imprisoned in the sun as we are in the cave,
They offer up the rusty execrations of the air
Against itself. They grind against its adamantine wall

And then are switched off like machines
Expelled from history they never know about.
And then they re-awake. They re-awake. They re-awake.

Your Kind of Town

This is the kind of drinking town
That does a lot of quiet service
Teaching people not to write.

Discuss the concept with a beer,
A fifth, the whole distillery.
The wives depart. They take your life

In suitcases in strangers' cars.
There are decisions to be made:
Go fishing, shoot yourself, or hit the bars.

A hard school, but you'd miss the camaraderie
Of other solitary egotists
Who like to think they keep the faith

And die a little faster every day
And one day don't show up. Let me get this.
Try as you may, you cannot stop. And now

Although your mind was somewhere else
It seems you went and wrote another book.
You live on Maker's Mark and Listerine,

Avoid advice and wake up in the dark
Beside a scream that claims you for its own.
It's always good to know you're not alone.

Scene of

February. The leaves turn white
from weariness at being dead.

The fences slump on bailer twine.
Fire in an oildrum, purpose unknown.

More birches and more fog
than all the bears in Canada

know what to do with.
To say nothing of the yellow-brown

moquette squalor of indoors,
where nothing works

but repetition: vodka,
child neglect and smack.

The place has spent a lifetime, several,
waiting for its murder.

You could call it a project.
Someone passing through

must grasp its real
potential, and the current

residents, yeah, they want it –
dead, be dead, be done with this.

Give it a week. If they could
ever concentrate they might

be dramatists themselves.
No matter: here it comes.

Meet the Monster

'Give me again / . . . the designer's sketches'

I ought to have been grateful. I was not.
The far side of the table kept insisting
As though I'd failed to grasp the urgency,
The need, the oh-so-human theme.
So something was amiss with me,
Rejecting first encouragement, then sympathy.
Because I did not share the overwhelming sense
That to emote like fuck was proof
Of deeper feeling, I must be
A monster and a shadow, one who merely
Watches others do the living for me –
Or maybe worse, too well brought up
To say that when you talk like this
You bore me, while the thing itself,
The shadow-stuff, the shadow-salt
That scalds the eyes and flays the tongue,
The shadow-milk winched up
In rusty buckets from a well of bile
And waiting on the step at dawn
Like life, cannot be simply named to suit
Your mood of anxious affirmation
Or a calendar of wishing. Oh my dears, in short,
The shadow-land with its ten thousand pits
Is not the place to do your fishing.

Anger

Scarcely are we introduced and you're in residence.
You say I know what's good for me. The light in here's
Too bright, so make it dingy, thirty watts, the Fifties,
With a smell of damp and cats and time gone bad. So can I feel
The imminence, a little bit? Just try and stop me. On the hour,
Somewhere upstairs, the argument that never ends is back,
Between the shouts of rage and the persistent quiet tone
That could provoke a murder, but not yet, because there is
A piece of this establishment that anger has not claimed
And has not found till now – a place to sit and listen, halfway
Up the stairs. You count the steps for me. That's right. From there
I get to exercise a choice and finally be overwhelmed
By my inheritance: so now the inexhaustible despair,
The whispers and the screams are mine. By day these lunatics
Are deadpan though dry-mouthed with rage. By night
They break new ground in the monotony of pain. But thank you
For advancing me this wisdom, which on second glance
Appears to be a debt that cannot be repaid, while I no longer
Occupy my body only, but a corner of this airless room
You've locked me in to celebrate the old religion too –
Its vinegar and loathing. Plenitude. So what's wrong now? I ask.
It's always you, you, you, you say. Why is that? Tell me. Tell me.

Metro Tunnel

Try not to get carried away when you enter
The foot-tunnel under the tracks. It's flooded
And full of weird shite – novels and jogging pants,
Tricycles, popsicles, animal bones
And breathless utterances addressed to brick.
You can see what might arise – there's murder, yes,
But also the attempt to make this ruined temple
Give up its secrets, any secret. So, unwary
And down here by accident, it could be
Agonizing to suppose this Untergang
Merely exemplifies thousands, with only
Minor local variations in the range of
Fetishes and discards on display: a plimsoll
And a ra-ra skirt are interchangeable; the cover
Of *Dusty in Memphis* in this dispensation belongs
Here beside Max Bygraves' later work, as no one
But a headcase could deny. Remember
How at all times we must bear in mind
That this is not the preface but the end.
New evidence will not have come to light. It's not
An opportunity for reconsideration.
Here among these sacred objects God is not
A detail or a faint aroma. He's just not.

Wood

But I moot been in prison thurgh Saturne,
And eke thurgh Juno, jalous and eek wood

There are no markers in the woods, the woods themselves
So old, so long sold off into disuse that what appears
To be a woodpile is a drift of fallen birches turning
On the air's slow tide, through which the tide's slow air
Is playing on repeat. This is the wood of the mad
Where under Saturn Palamon would ride,
With its limited palette, grey, brown, grey, grey-white,
Furnished like a secondary hell, its watercourses
Thick with time and halting altogether as they reach
The old sluice at the boundary where all this ends.
The path curves back towards the core, the wood's heart
Neither beating nor unbroken, when the air will pause,
Release itself across the dead white leaves
And having taken stock, be nowhere.

The Shirt of Nessus

He exits through the kitchen
Seeing no one, to the woods of boyhood
Where he means to blow his brains out.
This is in July. Among the trees
They have anticipated his intention.
He is relieved of his possessions
But will keep the Shirt of Nessus.
He writes letters to his wife,
And to his son in the inferno
That approaches from the east,
Then last his old professor, now retired
To a lake where he is watching
Barges dumping gold. The old man sends
His manservant and housekeeper
Away with thanks and blessings.
The prisoner sees this, sees all
The failures of the slow conspiracy.
Soon tanks will cross the Vistula.
He must write his other testament
On the insides of his eyelids,
Hoping that his eyes survive him
When his body is unearthed
Inside the prison yard by those
Who come a day, an hour too late,
But see smoke rising from the earth.
It may be so. And then
One autumn day he wakes inside

A state he cannot name, of knowing
Every scratch upon the iron door,
And all the names from which
The screams that rise all hours
From the sweat-soaked underworld
Have been detached. It smells,
He smells, of burning now.
The shirt of Nessus swarms
With self-consuming roses.
Yes, he writes, although his hands
Resemble candlewax that drips
To seal the page before his book
Is done, I think there is
Another place where we might live,
Beyond the lime-pits in the baking fields
Train after train is passing through
Ablaze and bound for nowhere.
And yet, he adds, black roses
Coiling from his eyes, to wait
Among the rags of time, and to lament,
Must be the only consolation.

The Golden Age

In the unselfconscious kingdom
Where vegetables vastly loved
Because that's what they're for —
It was the wish of the divine
That fig and cucumber entwine —
There was a gate, but nobody alas
Has found it since we found the means
To speak of gates, and love, and war.

That enviable greenness can't survive
The mind's eye where we treasure it
As evidence of how to live
Or might have lived, before.
The tempter comes to whisper
Measure it: to each his own,
To each her long submission
To the greater cause. My, how we've grown.

The Sea-Coast of Bohemia

From the distempered hallway you would hear
The alcoholic painter cursing overhead
That Clement Greenberg had him by the balls.
The girls all disappeared, except the proto-Goth
Who wouldn't play but hung her stockings on a line
Out back – *pour épater* your man, he would confide.
With all that the jism steaming of an afternoon,
And green infected sputum raining down,
Dispensed by the musicians up beneath the roof
Awaiting news of what to borrow next,
Was there enough to constitute a scene?
The time the horse went back upstairs and stopped
And shat outside the painter's door, it seemed
The building would collapse, as was foretold
The night that lavatory fell through the bathroom floor
With someone's pregnant girlfriend sat there skinning up.
Was this the *boue* they sought to be nostalgic for?
Or maybe just another in-between, a place to smoke
And drink and fuck and sulk until the signal changed
And carried them still further down the drain,
To Goole and Crowle and Bawtry where in God's name
Surely no one could be meant to live. All gone.
Except the painter who would die in bondage
To his art by courtesy of Buckfast, and the Goth
Who had a choice – découpage, or the fetish clubs
Down by the docks – and plumped for neither,
Waiting out the days before her broken mirror,
Wishing she was young and sinister again.

Blue Afternoons

i.m. Menno Wigman

Those were the afternoons. We let them go to waste.
To do so in a dim blue fog of Number 6 and Afghan Black
Seemed like a blow for freedom, so we struck it, smoked
And went on sitting there long after dark with three LPs
And a packet of skins with the cover torn off,
With aspirations and bronchitis, crablice and a chronic
Inability to put the empties on the step six feet away.
We worked with what there was to hand, so while the world
Lay all before us we could never find a use for it.
Then, later on, we died, three streets from where we sat,
The wrong side of the Hull with all the bridges burnt
And the survivors far too short of energy themselves
To stand and reminisce outside the crematorium
Or scatter us, though the scattering of ashes was an art
We'd all perfected privately, reclining long ago
On mangy sofas while the record jumped and no one could be
Arsed to deal with it. Those were the days. They really were.

Comedians

In memory of Mathew Sweeney

'*We were no good as murderers. We were clowns.*'
James Simmons

It was our last engagement in Berlin.
Once more as if by magic we stepped out
Through the curtains of Nebel und Nacht

To do our stuff and parley with the guard
On the gate at the British Army hotel
At which by some appalling stroke

Of dark absurdity we had been booked.
We stood there in our long black coats
And homburgs, with matching black holdalls.

The squaddie unshouldered his weapon
And rang in to summon assistance. So,
Should we read him a poem? Or do one

Back into the darkness? We waited,
Since waiting was what we did best.
We had out-bored a hundred terminals,

Born to the trade, man and boy, man and boy,
And as with Mike and Bernie you might ask:
So which one is meant to be funny?

Either, neither, both. We'd died a death
In halls from Magdeburg to Spandau
But our timing was uncanny, coming on

Like this and in this of all places,
Just as they winched the iron down for good
And closed the palace of varieties. At last

A sergeant came, a regular humourless
UnFalstaffian man, who could not tell
Which side if any we were on. For an age

He examined the passports, one red, one green,
Of Estragon Goldberg and Vladimir McCann.
For all I know we may be waiting still.

And There You Were

The streets were full of fallen leaves, the clocks were going back.
I was early for something, half-reading the paper,
The bar behind Euston packed out with the young after work.

I admired their laconic assignations.
I was not young. Nor, certainly, could you have been,
But before it could even seem strange, there you were.

The woman, a blonde, was charmed and ceasing to be watchful.
You were mid-anecdote, mid-apothegm, mid-joke, midway
To somewhere, neither old nor young but like yourself.

So, glancing up from time to time, you admired
The barmaid who had pinned her black hair up,
Admired shyly and in awe the white nape of her neck –

Which I'd heard you several times declare
The most beautiful thing about women.
And if your companion noticed, as surely she must have,

She seemed not to mind, having instantly come to accept
That being generous to a fault you must be shared.
Then as the bar emptied, long after I ought to have left,

You stayed on, confirming a purpose –
This and not some other place would be your destination
For the moment. And of course you didn't see me.

The tube-lines spread beneath your feet, the glasses
With a faint vibration went on sitting on their pools
Along the bar. That night the world was still in love with you

And had to claim you back again, since you were dead,
As I well knew, and your companion was there
For someone else, or never there at all,

But when you vanished and I made to leave
You lingered in the mirror for an eye-blink,
And again you didn't see me, but pausing where you stood

Gazed out into the future to beguile it, and there seemed
No doubt the future would require
Your presence as a charm against the dark.

The Rendezvous

I missed our rendezvous, James Wright, of course I did.
I was asleep, if you can call it sleep,
In a roomette bunk with North Dakota howling past.

I missed the snow-swept freight-yards
Where the northern railroads meet in one great chord
At Fargo, which you feared and loathed,

A city nowadays known if at all
For Steve Buscemi's booted leg
Protruding from the chipper into which

Peter Stormare has already fed the rest of him.
I won't debate you is Buscemi's final line. You said
You feared the War between the States

Made everyone secede from everyone:
Now multitudes within the multitude
Who have to live like things have learned to hate

All those with whom they share the gift of suffering.
And as I say, I missed the rendezvous,
But in the dream's eye I could see you

Strike a match against the engine's iron hide —
Show an affirming flame, as someone said,
And in that fearful blizzard.

But both of us were too far gone
And then the train swung southwards
Into Minnesota, and though it cried all night

It went unheard at William Duffy's farm
Where snow was burying the horses
And their treasury of dung.

Charlene the stern attendant woke us
Thirty minutes out from Minneapolis St Paul,
Twin cities which you knew as Hell

Through all those winters lost in Dinkytown
Among the legendary drunks.
When they denied you tenure finally

You lived with three shirts and one shoe,
A borrowed suitcase stuffed with symphonies
And a glass that concealed an invisible hole.

You broke new ground in being so far indisposed
That even Berryman was fit to deputize.
Down there in Hell the black Ohio

Secretly consumed the Mississippi
Every freezing night, and you alone could see
The blessed company of miners and their angel-whores

Who gathered on the burning shore to sing
The hymn they learned in grade school
Which was all that they possessed.

At journey's end I looked for you
At Union Depot, down the empty halls,
And in the bars and slaughter-yards

Above the river, and in the faces of the derelicts
Outside the library built by James J. Hill —
The very day they shut it down

And all the knowledge had to die. No luck,
And I am sorry I was late again
Though maybe what you had to share in sum

Was fear and solitude, which I have always known,
And anyway, as you were anxious to affirm,
The best is yet to come. Drink up.

Januarius

The two-faced god of gates and entrance-ways
Turns only one in your direction. He has other tasks
Requiring his disdain. He's never heard of you
And if there were a list your name would not be on it.
So you won't be going out. And anyway, where to?
You turn aside to find the gnomon risen halfway
From its clock of icy brass, as though the sword
That ought to save the nation is stuck fast,
With no explanatory literature to hand
But what you scrape like hard frost from a windscreen,
While the globe the sundial represents as flat
Has turned from verb to noun, from wintering to winter,
And will turn no longer. This must be the end –
The fixed stars glitter and Orion on his frieze of night
Is polishing his blade, aloof, peremptory
In his immobile progress down the darkened corridor
From 'nowhere into nowhere', with his cloak of ice
Flung out behind him like a comet's trail.
This can't be happening. It's not: but we were not designed
For stories with no deeds or conversation. Januarius,
Take pity. Tell us anything. A sad tale's best for winter.

Note on *Hammersmith*

In recent years a great many people have begun to investigate their family histories with the help of specialist websites and convenient software. Among the reasons for this are understandable curiosity, the desire to establish some facts, and the need to test the veracity of stories handed down. Ancestors underwrite our existence (so we assume, or hope) in a way we cannot quite do for ourselves. This seems more important as we grow older, although we risk dispelling some of the more romantic and agreeable tales and impressions that have come down to us. A couple of members of my own family are at work on genealogical projects of this kind, finding their way back to the soldiers of the Crimean War, or to Methodist missionaries working in the Pacific. I'm interested in what they discover, and in their absorption in it, but not in undertaking such investigations myself. So in one way it might seem odd to be writing a poem such as *Hammersmith*, which appears to depend on family history in order to exist.

Robert Lowell asked, 'Why not say what happened?' Good question. But *Hammersmith* is to a significant degree a work of the imagination. It's informed by things my parents told me about life in London in wartime and the early post-war years, and prompted by my memories, by walking about, by reading and film, but it makes no claims to documentary accuracy. It bears more resemblance to a dream than a factual record; its task is to evoke rather than sub-stantiate. Even if I wanted to write a chronicle I would be unable to do so, because my information is limited. There is a great deal I wasn't told or didn't ask about, and much of it is a material not encompassed by libraries or archives, things known only to those who were there at the time, almost all of whom are dead now. For the purposes of the imagination, I find that reconstruction does not fit the bill.

If *Hammersmith* can still in some sense be read as history, it is the history of an imagination. In the life of the imagination, matters which seem separable from each other in the waking world, such as historical and political facts, actual places and the forms and loca-tions they assume in reverie, personal impressions and memories, the known and the dreamed, appear to merge, shift and re-combine. There is an experience familiar in dreams, where an initial intention – perhaps the attempt to find or do or rectify something – is end-lessly deferred. In *Hammersmith*, the main speaker, who at times shifts into a related character called Ryan (himself perhaps an escapee from some earlier poems), repeatedly finds himself at a loss to continue whatever search he is pursuing among the streets, bars, dancehalls and demolished sites of Hammersmith. Hammersmith itself is where he is required to be, an inescapable place of return, but trails lead to other parts of London as well, in particular to the East End, where my mother began her teaching career during the Blitz. The speaker can never quite arrive, which makes a kind of sense to me, since although I was born in London I never feel entirely present there.

There are some parallels between Ryan's situation and that of an indigent, long-dead poet called Mulligan, who passes through the text during some later cantos, and who unhelpfully alludes to his unfinished and possibly lost poem about the Thames. Mulligan has some connections to Joxer Daly in O'Casey's *Juno and the Paycock*. My parents played Juno and Joxer in an amateur production of this play; in the poem their roles have a prophetic element, and a photo of my father from the time shows him as both handsome and a trouble in store; but the he and she of *Hammersmith* are to a large degree imagined characters, leading lives of their own suggested by the intersection of places and the occasional known event.

As to the beginnings of *Hammersmith,* after the death of my mother in 2007 I tried for some time to write about her, but I was stuck until a momentary encounter took place on a bus approaching Hammersmith Bridge from the Barnes side. I offered my seat to a very elderly lady, who told me with stern self-possession that thank you, she preferred to stand. From the window I could see Chiswick Mall, where my mother had often walked as a young woman and entertained the idea of living. The juxtaposition gave me the way into the poem, which is called 'Elegy'. Combined with remembered scenes set on and near the bridge from Jules Dassin's great post-war London movie, *Night and the City* (1950), it also seems to have set in train what eventually started to become *Hammersmith.*

Hammersmith is partly about London, but it is also about Englishness, or a version of it implanted at a very early age, in this case while listening to the radio with my mother as she did the ironing, particularly when the Boat Race or the Grand National were broadcast. These events – with the place names and the commentaries and the whole assumed life they invoked – were clearly of a special and definitive order of reality. Slightly later on I found out about reification, but the enchantment proved hard to dispel, and recently when one of the oarsmen in the Boat Race caught a crab and nearly went into the Thames, a whole set of associations – river,

[97]

radio, England, the war, my parents, Hammersmith – came to mind afresh, like an invitation that could not be refused, even though it led into the labyrinth where class, race, political disappointment and madness were also waiting.

ACKNOWLEDGEMENTS

Crossings: Poets Respond to the Art of Sean Scully, Enchiridion, *New Boots and Pantisocracies*, Newcastle Poetry Festival, *New Humanist, Poem, PN Review, Poetry Ireland Review, Poetry London, Scottish Review of Books, Spark, Stand, The Irish Times, Times Literary Supplement.*

Cantos I and II of *Hammersmith* were published as a chapbook by Hercules Editions in 2016.